# Rumi

The poems titles appearing in this collection have been added for identification, they were not originally so titled by Rumi.

ISBN: 1840137185

Copyright © Axiom Publishing, 2004.

This edition produced for Grange Books

An Imptint of Grange Books Plc
The Grange
Kingsnorth Industrial Estate
Hoo, nr. Rochester
Kent ME3 9ND
www.Grangebooks.co.uk

This book is copyright. Apart from any fair dealing for the purpose of private study, research, criticism or review, as permitted under the Copyright Act, no part may be reproduced by any process without written permission. Enquiries should be made to the publisher.

Printed in Malaysia

# Rumi

*Selections from the "Masnavi"
by Jalal Ad-Din Rumi*
Translated by E.H. Whinfield 1898

"Everything in the universe is a pitcher
brimming with wisdom and beauty."
— *Rumi*

# Content

| | |
|---|---|
| **Introduction** | 8 |
| **Power Of The Soul** | 9 |
| **Greed** | 10 |
| **Sun Of The Soul** | 11 |
| **Voyage** | 12 |
| **Mysteries Of The Gospel** | 13 |
| **The Believer's Heart** | 14 |
| **Earth-Born/Heaven-Born** | 15 |
| **Water** | 16 |
| **The Philosophy** | 17 |
| **Love's Treasure** | 18 |
| **Trust** | 19 |
| **The Knowledge Of Men** | 20 |
| **Counsels To Zaid** | 22 |
| **Expression** | 23 |
| **Forbidden Fruits** | 24 |
| **Knowledge And Opinion** | 26 |
| **The Holy Words** | 27 |
| **The Evolution Of Man** | 28 |
| **Think Not Yourself Perfect** | 30 |
| **Gaze** | 31 |
| **Sometime Thoughts** | 32 |
| **Every Moment A Fresh Purpose** | 33 |
| **Soul And Body** | 34 |
| **Lesson Of The Rose** | 35 |
| **Paradise** | 36 |
| **To Die And Rise** | 37 |

| | |
|---|---|
| Hidden Power | 38 |
| The Beloved's Love | 39 |
| Through Love | 40 |
| With Thee | 41 |
| The Good And Bad | 42 |
| Women's Wiles | 43 |
| Pain | 44 |
| Mercy | 45 |
| From Him | 46 |
| The Second Lough | 47 |
| Two At The Mosque | 48 |
| Subject And Predicate | 49 |
| Infant Thoughts | 50 |
| The Read-flute | 51 |
| Resurrection Day | 52 |
| The Eye And the Ear | 53 |
| Reason | 54 |
| This Truth And That Truth | 55 |
| Rust On Rust | 56 |
| Light | 57 |
| Voices | 58 |
| Tree Of Knowledge | 60 |
| Ducks | 61 |
| The Smell Of Evil Deeds | 62 |
| From Reason And Mind | 63 |
| The Seeker | 64 |
| Evil Doubts, Evil Friends | 66 |

| | |
|---|---|
| My Companions, The Stars | 67 |
| The Snake | 68 |
| Lost In The Evil Spirit | 70 |
| From One Danger To A Worse | 71 |
| Infidelity | 72 |
| Black And White | 73 |
| Abstinence | 74 |
| 'Tis I | 75 |
| Regrets | 76 |
| No Chain Binds Him | 77 |
| The Garden Knows | 78 |
| Weeds On Water | 80 |
| I Know Not | 81 |
| Tear Not Thy Plumage Off | 82 |
| One Religion | 83 |
| God The Creator | 84 |
| Awakening | 85 |
| Release From Danger | 86 |
| Right Uses | 87 |
| Soul's Awakening | 88 |
| Sleepers | 89 |
| Banishing Fears | 90 |
| Tree Of Man | 91 |
| Taught Be God | 92 |
| Secret Sins | 93 |
| Colours And Light | 94 |
| Potherbs | 95 |

| | |
|---|---|
| Painting On A Wall | 96 |
| The Work Of Each | 97 |
| God Speaks | 98 |
| Reasons | 100 |
| Sent From Heaven | 101 |
| The Prophet Said... | 102 |
| No Absolutes | 103 |
| Love | 104 |
| The Spheres' Song | 105 |
| Fearless Love | 106 |
| Black Coal | 107 |
| Bad Friends | 108 |
| Journeying | 109 |
| The Thirst And The Water | 110 |
| Battling Against Advise | 111 |
| The Tree Is Born From The Fruit | 112 |
| The Love Of The Soul | 113 |
| Chains | 114 |
| God's Servants | 115 |
| Sight Restored | 116 |
| Hidden Treasure | 117 |
| The Tree Counsels | 118 |
| The World Is Transitory | 120 |
| True Reason | 122 |
| Food For The Soul | 124 |
| To The Birds | 125 |
| Ready Cash | 126 |

## Introduction

The greatest mystical poet of Persia, Rumi, was born on September 29, 1207, not in Persia but in a north-eastern province of present day Afghanistan. At the age of 12, he and his family went first to Mecca after fleeing the Mongol invasion, before settling in the town of Konya in 1228.

At age 37 Rumi met a wandering dervish, a holy man named Shams al-Din who seemed to Rumi the perfect and complete man, the image of the "Divine Beloved", and through this meeting was introduced into the mystical path of the Sufi tradition. Rumi studied in Aleppo and Damascus and himself became a Sufi teacher, and due to his eloquence, theological knowledge and personality, gathered within a few years his own group of disciples. In 1247 Rumi withdrew from his disciples and devoted himself to Shams. In an attempt to regain Rumi's attention some of his own followers and students murdered Shams. Rumi was overwhelmed with grief and withdrew from the world. He began to realise a great love of God and expressed this devotion through his beautiful poetry.

For the next twenty-five years Rumi's output was staggering as he composed almost 30,000 rhyming couplets, odes and quatrains.

The poetry of Rumi teaches that only through love may the way to spiritual growth and insight be found.

On the evening of December 17, 1273 Rumi passed from life into death. This time is now known as his 'wedding night,' for his followers believe he was, that night, completely united with God.

## Power Of The Soul

As in oyster-shells raindrops are pearls.
Outside the shell they are raindrops, great and small;
Inside they are precious pearls, big and little.
These men also resemble the musk deer's bag;
Outside it is blood, but inside pure musk;
Yet, say not that outside 'twas mere blood,
Which on entering the bag becomes musk.
Nor say that outside the alembic 'twas mere copper,
And becomes gold inside, when mixed with elixir.
In you freewill and compulsion are vain fancies,
But in them they are the light of Almighty power.
On the table bread is a mere lifeless thing,
When taken into the body it is a life-giving spirit.
This transmutation occurs not in the table's heart,
'Tis soul effects this transmutation with water of life.
Such is the power of the soul, O man of right views!
Then what is the power of the Soul of souls?

*Masnavi— Book 1: 6*

# Greed

Would you have eyes and ears of reason clear,
Tear off the obstructing veil of greed!
The blind imitation of that Sufi proceeded from greed;
Greed closed his mind to the pure light.
Yea, 'twas greed that led astray that Sufi,
And brought him to loss of property and ruin.
Greed of victuals, greed of that ecstatic singing
Hindered his wits from grasping the truth.
If greed stained the face of a mirror,
That mirror would be as deceitful as we men are.
If a pair of scales were greedy of riches,
Would they tell truly the weight of anything?

*Masnavi— Book 2: 1*

## Sun Of The Soul

Shadows induce slumber, like evening talks,
But when the sun arises the "moon is split asunder."
In the world there is naught so wondrous as the sun,
But the Sun of the soul sets not and has no yesterday.
Though the material sun is unique and single,
We can conceive similar suns like to it.
But the Sun of the soul, beyond this firmament,
No like thereof is seen in concrete or abstract.

*Masnavi— Book 1: 1*

# Voyage

When you place goods upon a ship,
You do it in trust that the voyage will be prosperous;
You know not which of the two events will befall you,
Whether you will be drowned or come safe to land.
If you say, 'Till I know which will be my fate
I will not set foot upon the ship;
Shall I be drowned on the voyage or a survivor?
Reveal to me in which class I shall be.
I shall not undertake the voyage on the chance
On the bare hope of reaching land, as the rest do.'
In that case no trade at all will be undertaken by you,
As the secret of these two events is always hidden.
The lamp of the heart, that is a timid trader,
Acquires neither loss nor gain by its ventures.

*Masnavi*— Book 3: 13

## Mysteries Of The Gospel

**M**yriads of Christians flocked round him,
One after another they assembled in his street.
Then he would preach to them of mysteries,
Mysteries of the Gospel, of stoles, of prayers.
He would preach to them with eloquent words
Concerning the words and acts of the Messiah.

*Masnavi— Book 1: 3*

# The Believer's Heart

The Prophet said that God has declared,
"I am not contained in aught above or below,
I am not contained in earth or sky, or even
In highest heaven. Know this for a surety. O beloved!
Yet am I contained in the believer's heart!
If ye seek me, search in such hearts!"

*Masnavi— Book 1: 9*

*Rumi*

# Earth-Born/Heaven-Born

O Thou that changest earth into gold,
And out of other earth madest the father of mankind,
Thy business is changing things and bestowing favours,
My business is mistakes and forgetfulness and error.
Change my mistakes and forgetfulness to knowledge;
I am altogether vile, make me temperate and meek.
O Thou that convertest salt earth into bread,
And bread again into the life of men;
Thou who madest the erring soul a guide to men,
And him that erred from the way a prophet;
Thou makest some earth-born men as heaven,
And multipliest heaven-born saints on earth!

*Masnavi— Book 5: 3*

# Water

The eye of outward sense is as the palm of a hand,
The whole of the object is not grasped in the palm.
The sea itself is one thing, the foam another;
Neglect the foam, and regard the sea with your eyes.
Waves of foam rise from the sea night and day,
You look at the foam ripples and not the mighty sea.
We, like boats, are tossed hither and thither,
We are blind though we are on the bright ocean.
Ah! you who are asleep in the boat of the body,
You see the water; behold the Water of waters!
Under the water you see there is another Water moving it,
Within the spirit is a Spirit that calls it.

*Masnavi— Book 3: 5*

# The Philosopher

The philosopher denies the existence of the Devil;
At the same time he is the Devil's laughing-stock.
If thou hast not seen the Devil, look at thyself,
Without demon's aid how came that blue turban on thy brow?
Whosoever has a doubt or disquietude in his heart
Is a secret denier and philosopher.
Now and then he displays firm belief,
But that slight dash of philosophy blackens his face.
Beware, O believers! That lurks in you too;
You may develop innumerable states of mind.
(Blue turbans were considered a sign of hypocrisy)

*Masnavi*— Book 1: 13

## Love's Treasure

Through love bewilderment befalls the power of speech,
It no longer dares to utter what passes;
For if it sets forth an answer, it fears greatly
That its secret treasure may escape its lips.
Therefore it closes lips from saying good or bad,
So that its treasure may not escape it.

*Masnavi— Book 5: 11*

## Trust

Trust in God, as opposed to human exertions.
The beasts said, "O enlightened sage,
Lay aside caution; it cannot help thee against destiny;
To worry with precaution is toil and moil;
Go, trust in Providence, trust is the better part.
War not with the divine decree, O hot-headed one,
Lest that decree enter into conflict with thee.
Man should be as dead before the commands of God
Lest a blow befall him from the Lord of all creatures."
He said, "True; but though trust be our mainstay,
Yet the Prophet teaches us to have regard to means."
The Prophet cried with a loud voice,
"Trust in God, yet tie the camel's leg."

*Masnavi— Book 1: 5*

## The Knowledge Of Men

The knowledge of men of heart bears them up,
The knowledge of men of the body weighs them down.
When 'tis knowledge of the heart, it is a friend;
When knowledge of the body, it is a burden.
God saith, "As an ass bearing a load of books,"
The knowledge which is not of Him is a burden.
Knowledge which comes not immediately from Him
Endures no longer than the rouge of the tirewoman.
Nevertheless, if you bear this burden in a right spirit
'Twill be removed, and you will obtain joy.
See you bear not that burden out of vainglory,
Then you will behold a store of true knowledge within.
When you mount the steed of this true knowledge,
Straightway the burden will fall from your back.
If you drink not His cup, how will you escape lusts?
You, who seek no more of Him than to name His name?
What do His name and fame suggest? The idea of Him.
And the idea of Him guides you to union with Him.
Know you a guide without something to which it guides?
Were there no roads there would be no ghouls.
Know you a name without a thing answering to it?
Have you ever plucked a rose from Gaf and Lam?
You name His name; go, seek the reality named by it!
Look for the moon in heaven, not in the water!
If you desire to rise above mere names and letters,
Make yourself free from self at one stroke!

Like a sword be without trace of soft iron;
Like a steel mirror, scour off all rust with contrition;
Make yourself pure from all attributes of self,
That you may see your own pure bright essence!
Yea, see in your heart the knowledge of the Prophet,
Without book, without tutor, without preceptor.
The Prophet saith, "He is one of my people,
Whoso is of like temper and spirit with me.
His soul beholds me by the selfsame light
Whereby I myself behold him,
Without traditions and scriptures and histories,
In the fount of the water of life."

*Masnavi*— Book 1: 14

# Counsels To Zaid

Counsels of Reserve given by the Prophet to his Freedman Zaid.
At dawn the Prophet said to Zaid,
"How is it with thee this morning, O pure disciple?"
He replied, "Thy faithful slave am I." Again he said,
"If the garden of faith has bloomed, show a token of it."
He answered, "I was athirst many days,
By night I slept not for the burning pangs of love;
So that I passed by days and nights,
As the point of a spear glances off a shield.
For in that state all faith is one,
A hundred thousand years and a moment are all one;
World without beginning and world without end are one;
Reason finds no entrance when mind is thus lost."

*Masnavi*— Book 1: 15

## Expression

Every expression is the sign of a state of mind;
That state is a hand, the expression an instrument.
A goldsmith's instruments in the hand of a cobbler
Are as grains of wheat sown on sand.
The tools of a cobbler in the hand of a cultivator
Are as grass before a dog or bones before an ass.

For he who is ignorant misuses the instrument ;
If you strike flint on mud you will get no fire.
Hand and instrument resemble flint and steel;
You must have a pair; a pair is needed to generate.

*Masnavi— Book 2: 1*

## Forbidden Fruits

Alas! the forbidden fruits were eaten,
And thereby the warm life of reason was congealed.
A grain of wheat eclipsed the sun Of Adam,
Like as the Dragon's tail dulls the brightness of the moon.
Behold how delicate is the heart, that a morsel of dust
Clouded its moon with foul obscurity!
When bread is "substance," to eat it nourishes us;
When 'tis empty "form," it profits nothing.
Like as the green thorn which is cropped by the camel,
And then yields him pleasure and nutriment;
When its greenness has gone and it becomes dry,
If the camel crops that same thorn in the desert,
It wounds his palate and mouth without pity,
As if conserve of roses should turn to sharp swords.
When bread is "substance," it is as a green thorn;
When 'tis "form," 'tis as the dry and coarse thorn.
And thou eatest it in the same way as of yore
Thou wert wont to eat it, O helpless being,
Eatest this dry thing in the same manner,
After the real "substance" is mingled with dust;
It has become mingled with dust, dry in pith and rind.
O camel, now beware of that herb!
The Word is become foul with mingled earth;
The water is become muddy; close the mouth of the well,
Till God makes it again pure and sweet;
Yea, till He purifies what He has made foul.

Patience will accomplish thy desire, not haste.
Be patient, God knows what is best.
(Muhammadans think the forbidden fruit to have been wheat.)

*Masnavi— Book 1: Epilogue*

## Knowledge And Opinion

Knowledge has two wings, opinion only one wing;
Opinion is weak and lopsided in its flight.
The bird having but one wing quickly drops down,
And again flies on two steps or more.
This bird of opinion goes on rising and falling
On one wing, in hope to reach his nest.
When he escapes from opinion and knowledge is seen,
This bird gains two wings and spreads both of them.

*Masnavi*— Book 3: 7

## The Holy Words

Many are the holy words that find no entrance
Into blind hearts, but they enter hearts full of light.
But the deceits of Satan enter crooked hearts,
Even as crooked shoes fit crooked feet.
Though you repeat pious expressions again and again,
If you are a fool, they affect you not at all;
Nay, not though you set them down in writing,
And though you proclaim them vauntingly;
Wisdom averts its face from you, O man of sin,
Wisdom breaks away from you and takes to flight!

*Masnavi— Book 2: 1*

## The Evolution Of Man

First he appeared in the class of inorganic things,
Next he passed therefrom into that of plants.
For years he lived as one of the plants,
Remembering naught of his inorganic state so different;
And when he passed from the vegetive to the animal state
He had no remembrance of his state as a plant,
Except the inclination he felt to the world of plants,
Especially at the time of spring and sweet flowers.
Like the inclination of infants towards their mothers,
Which know not the cause of their inclination to the breast,
Or the excessive inclination of young disciples
Towards their noble and illustrious teachers.
The disciple's partial reason comes from that Reason,
The disciple's shadow is from that bough.
When the shadows in the disciples cease,
They know the reason of their attachment to the teachers.
For, O fortunate one, how can the shadow move,
Unless the tree that casts the shadow move as well?
Again, the great Creator, as you know,
Drew man out of the animal into the human state.
Thus man passed from one order of nature to another,
Till he became wise and knowing and strong as he is now.
Of his first souls he has now no remembrance,
And he will be again changed from his present soul.
In order to escape from his present soul full of lusts
He must behold thousands of reasonable souls.

Though man fell asleep and forgot his previous states,
Yet God will not leave him in this self-forgetfulness;
And then he will laugh at his own former state
Saying, " What mattered my experiences when asleep?
When I had forgotten my prosperous condition,
And knew not that the grief and ills I experienced
Were the effect of sleep and illusion and fancy?
In like manner this world, which is only a dream.
Seems to the sleeper as a thing enduring for ever
But when the morn of the last day shall dawn,
The sleeper will escape from the cloud of illusion;
Laughter will overpower him at his own fancied grieves
When he beholds his abiding home and place.
Whatever you see in this sleep, both good and evil,
Will all be exposed to view on the resurrection day.
Whatever you have done during your sleep in the world
Will be displayed to you clearly when you awake.
Imagine not that these ill deeds of yours exist not
In this sleep of yours, and will not be revealed to you.

*Masnavi— Book 4: 9*

## Think Not Yourself Perfect

When a garment is made by a good tailor,
'Tis an evidence of the tailor's art.
Logs of wood would not be duly shaped
Did not the carpenter plan outline and detail.
The leech skilled in setting bones goes
Where lies the patient with a broken leg.
If there were no sick and infirm,
How could the excellence of the leech's art be seen?
If vile base copper were not mingled,
How could the alchemist show his skill?
Defects are the mirrors of the attributes of Beauty,
The base is the mirror of the High and Glorious One,
Because one contrary shows forth its contrary,
As honey's sweetness is shown by vinegar's sourness.
Whoso recognises and confesses his own defects
Is hastening in the way that leads to perfection!
But he advances not towards the Almighty
Who fancies himself to be perfect.
No sickness worse than fancying thyself perfect
Can infect thy soul, O arrogant misguided one!
Shed many tears of blood from eyes and heart,
That this self-satisfaction may be driven out.
The fault of Iblis lay in saying, "I am better than he,"
And this same weakness lurks in the soul of all creatures.

*Book 1: 11*

# Gaze

Gaze not on your own pictures, fair or ugly,
Gaze on your love and the object of your desire.
Gaze not at the sight of your own weakness or vileness,
Gaze at object of your desire, O exalted one.

*Masnavi— Book 3: 6*

## Sometime Thoughts

From your thoughts proceeds destruction,
When from time to time evil thoughts occur to you.
Sometimes thoughts of pleasure, sometimes of business,
Sometimes thoughts of science, sometimes of house and home.
Sometimes thoughts of gain and traffic,
Sometimes thoughts of merchandise and wealth.
Sometimes thoughts of money and wives and children,
Sometimes thoughts of wisdom or of sadness.
Sometimes thoughts of household goods and fine linen,
Sometimes thoughts of carpets, sometimes of sweepers.
Sometimes thoughts of mills, gardens, and villas,
Sometimes of clouds and mists and jokes and jests.
Sometimes thoughts of peace and war,
Sometimes thoughts of honour and disgrace.
Ah! cast out of your head these vain imaginations,
Ah! sweep out of your heart these evil suggestions.
Cry, "There is no power nor strength but in God!"

*Masnavi*— Book 2: 2

## Every Moment A Fresh Purpose

Every moment I impart a fresh bias to the heart,
Every instant I set a fresh mark on the heart;
Each day I am engaged in a fresh work,
There is naught that swerves from my purpose."
There is a tradition, "The heart is like a feather
In the desert, which is borne captive by the winds;
The wind drives it everywhere at random,
Now to right and now to left in opposite directions."
According to another tradition, know the heart is like
To water in a kettle boiling on the fire.
So every moment a fresh purpose occurs to the heart,
Not proceeding from itself, but from its situation.
Why, then, are you confident about the heart's purposes?
Why make you vows only to be covered with shame?

*Masnavi— Book 3: 9*

## Soul And Body

That my outward form may not mislead you,
Digest my sweet advice before copying me.
Many are they who have been captured by form,
Who aimed at form, and found Allah.
After all, soul is linked to body,
Though it in nowise resembles the body.
The power of the light of the eye is mated with fat,
The light of the heart is hidden in a drop of blood.
Joy harbours in the kidneys and pain in the liver,
The lamp of reason in the brains of the head;
Smell in the nostrils and speech in the tongue,
Concupiscence in the flesh and courage in the heart.
These connections are not without a why and a how,
But reason is at a loss to understand the how.
Universal Soul had connection with Partial Soul,
Which thence conceived a pearl and retained it in its bosom.
From that connection, like Mary,
Soul became pregnant of a fair Messiah;
Not that Messiah who walked upon earth and water,
But that Messiah who is higher than space.
Next, as Soul became pregnant by the Soul of souls,
So by the former Soul did the world become pregnant;
Then the World brought forth another world,
And of this last are brought forth other worlds.
Should I reckon them in my speech till the last day
I should fail to tell the total of these resurrections.

*Masnavi— Book 2: 4*

# Lesson Of The Rose

When sudden misfortunes befall thee.
Let others grow pale from fear of ill fortune,
Do thou smile like the rose at loss and gain;
For the rose, though its petals be torn asunder,
Still smiles on, and it is never cast down.
It says, "Why should I fall into grief in disgrace?
I gather beauty even from the thorn of disgrace."
Whatsoever is lost to thee through God's decree
Know of a surety is so much gained from misfortune.

*Masnavi— Book 3: 14*

# Paradise

A damsel said to her lover, "O fond youth,
You have visited many cities in your travels;
Which of those cities seems most delightful to you?"
He made answer, "The city wherein my love dwells.
In whatever nook my queen alights,
Though it be as the eye of a needle, 'tis a wide plain;
Wherever her Yusuf-like face shines as a moon,
Though it be the bottom of a well, 'tis Paradise."

*Masnavi— Book 3: 17*

## To Die And Rise

I died as inanimate matter and arose a plant,
I died as a plant and rose again an animal.
I died as an animal and arose a man.
Why then should I fear to become less by dying?
I shall die once again as a man
To rise an angel perfect from head to foot!

*Masnavi— Book 3: 17*

# Hidden Power

This world is ruled by a hidden Power.
It confesses its impotence before that hidden Power,
Which sometimes exalts it and sometimes lays it low,
Sometimes makes it dry and sometimes moist.
The hand is hidden, yet we see the pen writing;
The horse is galloping, yet the rider is hid from view.
The arrow speeds forth, yet the bow is not seen;
Souls are seen, the Soul of souls (God) is hidden.

*Masnavi— Book 2: 5*

# The Beloved's Love

No lover ever seeks union with his beloved,
But his beloved is also seeking union with him.
But the lover's love makes his body lean,
While the beloved's love makes hers fair and lusty.
When in this heart the lightning spark of love arises,
Be sure this love is reciprocated in that heart.

*Masnavi— Book 3: 17*

## Through Love

Love endures hardships at the hands of the Beloved.
Through love bitter things seem sweet,
Through love bits of copper are made gold.
Through love dregs taste like pure wine,
Through love pains are as healing balms.
Through love thorns become roses,
And through love vinegar becomes sweet wine.
Through love the stake becomes a throne,
Through love reverse of fortune seems good fortune.
Through love a prison seems a rose bower,
Without love a grate full of ashes seems a garden.
Through love burning fire is pleasing light,
Through love the Devil becomes a Houri.
Through love hard stones become soft as butter,
Without love soft wax becomes hard iron.
Through love grief is as joy,
Through love Ghouls turn into angels.
...Through love sickness is health,
Through love wrath is as mercy.
Through love the dead rise to life,
Through love the king becomes a slave.
Even when an evil befalls you, have due regard;
Regard well him who does you this ill turn.
The sight which regards the ebb and flow of good and ill
Opens a passage for you from misfortune to happiness.

*Masnavi*— Book 2: 6

# With Thee

With thee, my love, hell itself were heaven,
With thee a prison would be a rose-garden.
With thee hell would be a mansion of delight,
Without thee lilies and roses would be as flames of fire!

*Masnavi— Book 3: 17*

# The Good And Bad

A voice came from God to Moses,
"Why hast thou sent my servant away?
Thou hast come to draw men to union with me,
Not to drive them far away from me.
So far as possible, engage not in dissevering;
'The thing most repugnant to me is divorce.'
To each person have I allotted peculiar forms,
To each have I given particular usages.
What is praiseworthy in thee is blameable in him,
What is poison for thee is honey for him.
What is good in him is bad in thee,
What is fair in him is repulsive in thee.
I am exempt from all purity and impurity,
I need not the laziness or alacrity of my people.
I created not men to gain a profit from them,
But to shower my beneficence upon them."

*Masnavi— Book 2: 7*

## Women's Wiles

Men subdued by women's wiles.
In this manner she pleaded with gentle coaxing,
The while her tears fell upon her cheeks.
How could his firmness and endurance abide
When even without tears she could charm his heart?
That rain brought forth a flash of lightning
Which kindled a spark in the heart of that poor man.
Since the man was the slave of her fair face,
How was it when she stooped to slavish entreaties?
When she whose airs set thy heart a-quaking,
When she weeps, how feelest thou then?
When she whose coquetry makes thy heart bleed
Condescends to entreaties, how is it then?
She who subdues us with her pride and severity,
What plea is left us when she begins to plead?
When she who traded in naught but bloodshed
Submits at last, ah! what a profit she makes!

*Masnavi— Book 1: 9*

## Pain

Pain is a treasure, for it contains mercies;
The kernel is soft when the rind is scraped off.
O brother, the place of darkness and cold
Is the fountain of life and the cup of ecstasy.
So also is endurance of pain and sickness and disease.
For from abasement proceeds exaltation.
The spring seasons are hidden in the autumns,
And autumns are charged with springs; flee them not.
Consort with grief and put up with sadness,
Seek long life in your own death!

*Masnavi— Book 2: 10*

# Mercy

He who needs mercy finds it.
Doing kindness is the game and quarry of good men,
A good man seeks in the world only pains to cure.
Wherever there is a pain there goes the remedy,
Wherever there is poverty there goes relief.
Seek not water, only show you are thirsty,
That water may spring up all around you.

Be athirst! Allah knows what is best for you.
Seek you the water of mercy? Be downcast,
And straightway drink the wine of mercy to intoxication.

*Masnavi— Book 2: 8*

## From Him

Yea, all the fish in the seas,
And all feathered fowl in the air above,
All elephants, wolves, and lions of the forest,
All dragons and snakes, and even little ants,
Yea, even air, water, earth, and fire,
Draw their sustenance from Him, both winter and summer.
Every moment this heaven cries to Him, saying,
"O Lord, quit not Thy hold of me for a moment!
The pillar of my being is Thy aid and protection;
The whole is folded up in that right hand of Thine."
And earth cries, "O keep me fixed and steadfast,
Thou who hast placed me on the top of waters!"
All of them are waiting and expecting His aid,
All have learned of Him to represent their needs.
Every prophet extols this prescription,
"Seek ye help with patience and with prayer."
Ho! seek aid of Him, not of another than Him
Seek water in the ocean, not in a dried-up channel.

*Masnavi— Book 4: 2*

## The Second Laugh

When a friend tells a joke to his friend,
The deaf man who listens laughs twice over;
The first time from imitation and foolishness,
Because he sees all the party laughing;
Yet, though he laughs like the others,
He is then ignorant of the subject of their laughter;
Then he inquires what the laughter was about,
And, on hearing it, proceeds to laugh a second time.

*Masnavi— Book 5: 6*

## Two At The Mosque

A certain man was going into the mosque,
Just as another was coming out.
He inquired of him what had occurred to the meeting,
That the people were coming out of the mosque so soon.
The other told him that the Prophet
Had concluded the public prayers and mysteries.
"Whither go you," said he, "O foolish one,
Seeing the Prophet has already given the blessing?"
The first heaved a sigh, and its smoke ascended;
That sigh yielded a perfume of his heart's blood.
The other, who came from the mosque, said to him,
"Give me that sigh, and take my prayers instead."
The first said, "I give it, and take your prayers."
The other took that sigh with a hundred thanks.
He went his way with deep humility and contrition,
As a hawk who had ascended in the track of the falcon.
That night, as ho lay asleep, he heard a voice from heaven,
"Thou hast bought the water of life and healing;
The worth of what thou hast chosen and possessed
Equals that of all the people's accepted prayers."

*Masnavi— Book 2: 11*

## Subject And Predicate

When there is no subject,
The existence of a predicate is not possible.
When thou endurest not the pains of abstinence
And fulfillest not the terms, thou gainest no reward.
How easy those terms! how abundant that reward!
A reward that enchants the heart and charms the soul!

*Masnavi— Book 5: 3*

## Infant Thoughts

How can an infant on the road know the thoughts of men?
How far its fancies are removed from true knowledge!
The thoughts of infants run on the nurse and milk,
Or on raisins or nuts, or on crying and wailing.
The blind imitator is like a feeble infant,
Even though he possesses fine arguments and proofs.
His preoccupation with obscure arguments and proofs
Drags him away from insight into truth.
His stock of lore, which is the salve of his eyes,
Bears him off and plunges him in difficult questions.

*Masnavi— Book 5: 6*

## The Reed-flute

Hearken to the reed-flute, how it complains,
Lamenting its banishment from its home:
"Ever since they tore me from my osier bed,
My plaintive notes have moved men and women to tears.
I burst my breast, striving to give vent to sighs,
And to express the pangs of my yearning for my home.
He who abides far away from his home
Is ever longing for the day he shall return.
My wailing is heard in every throng,
In concert with them that rejoice and them that weep.
Each interprets my notes in harmony with his own feelings,
But not one fathoms the secrets of my heart.
My secrets are not alien from my plaintive notes,
Yet they are not manifest to the sensual eye and ear.
Body is not veiled from soul, neither soul from body,
Yet no man hath ever seen a soul."
This plaint of the flute is fire, not mere air.
Let him who lacks this fire be accounted dead!
'Tis the fire of love that inspires the flute,
'Tis the ferment of love that possesses the wine.
The flute is the confidant of all unhappy lovers;
Yea, its strains lay bare my inmost secrets.

*Masnavi— Book 1: Prologue*

## Resurrection Day

On the resurrection day all secrets will be disclosed;
Yea, every guilty one will be convicted by himself.
Hand and foot will bear testimony openly
Before the Almighty concerning their owner's sins.
Hand will say, "I stole such and such things;"
Lip will say, "I asked for such and such things."
Foot will say, "I went after my own desires;"
Arm will say, "I embraced the harlot."
Eye will say, "I looked after forbidden things;"
Ear will say, "I listened to evil talk."
Thus the man will be shown to be a liar from head to foot,
Since his own members will prove him to be a liar.

*Masnavi— Book 5: 9*

# The Eye And The Ear

"O sage, what is true and what is false?"
The sage touched his ear and said, "This is false,
But the eye is true and its report is certain."
The ear is false in relation to the eye,
And most assertions are related to the ear.
If a bat turn away its eyes from the sun,
Still it is not veiled from some idea of the sun;
Its very dread of the sun frames an idea of the sun,
And that idea scares it away to the darkness.
That idea of light terrifies it,
And makes it cling to the murky night.
Just so 'tis your idea of your terrible foe
Which makes you cling to your friends and allies.

*Masnavi— Book 5: 12*

# Reason

"If there were aught beyond this life we should see it."
But if the child sees not the state of reason,
Does the man of reason therefore forsake reason?
And if the man of reason sees not the state of love,
Is the blessed moon of love thereby eclipsed?

*Masnavi— Book 5: 12*

# This Truth And That Truth

All false doctrines contain an element of truth.
Just so every one in matters of doctrine
Gives a different description of the hidden subject.
A philosopher expounds it in one way,
And a critic at once refutes his propositions.
A third censures both of them;
A fourth spends his life in traducing the others.
Every one mentions indications of this road,
In order to create an impression that he has gone it.
This truth and that truth cannot be all true,
And yet all of them are not entirely astray in error.
Because error occurs not without some truth,
Fools buy base coins from their likeness to real coins.
If there were no genuine coins current in the world,
How could coiners succeed in passing false coins?
If there were no truth, how could falsehood exist?
Falsehood derives its plausibility from truth.
'Tis the desire of right that makes men buy wrong;
Let poison be mixed with sugar, and they eat it at once.
If wheat were not valued as sweet and good for food,
The cheat who shows wheat and sells barley would make no profit!
Say not, then, that all these creeds are false,
The false ones ensnare hearts by the scent of truth.
Say not that they are all erroneous fancies,
There is no fancy in the universe without some truth.

*Masnavi— Book 2: 11*

## Rust On Rust

On thy heart is rust on rust collected,
So thou art blind to mysteries.
Thy rust, layer on layer, O black kettle!
Makes the aspect of thy inner parts foul.
If that smoke touched a new kettle,
It would show the smut, were it only as a grain of barley;
For everything is made manifest by its opposite,
In contrast with its whiteness that black shows foul.
But when the kettle is black, then afterwards
Who can see on it the impression of the smoke?

*Masnavi— Book 2: 15*

# Light

You are bound to the bosom of earth like seeds,
Strive to be weaned through nutriment of the heart.
Eat the words of wisdom, for veiled light
Is not accepted in preference to unveiled light.
When you have accepted the light, O beloved,
When you behold what is veiled without a veil,
Like a star you will walk upon the heavens;
Nay, though not in heaven, you will walk on high.
Keep silence, that you may hear Him speaking
Words unutterable by tongue in speech.
Keep silence, that you may hear from that Sun
Things inexpressible in books and discourses.
Keep silence, that the Spirit may speak to you.

*Masnavi*— Book 3: 5

## Voices

"If you are a true lover of my soul,
This truth-fraught saying of mine is no vain pretence,
'Though I talk half the night I am superior to you;'
And again, 'Fear not the night; here am I, your kinsman.'
These two assertions of mine will both seem true to you
The moment you recognise the voice of your kinsman.
Superiority and kinsmanship are both mere assertions,
Yet both are recognised for truth by men of clear wit.
The nearness of the voice proves to such an one
That the voice proceeds from a friend who is near.
The sweetness of the kinsman's voice, too, O beloved,
Proves the veracity of that kinsman.
But the uninspired fool who from ignorance
Cannot tell the voice of a stranger from a friend's,
To him the friend's saying seems a vain pretension,
His ignorance is the material cause of his disbelief.
To the wise, whose hearts are enlightened,
The mere sound of that voice proves its truth."
"When you say to a thirsty man, 'Come quickly;
This is water in the cup, take and drink it,'
Does the thirsty man say, 'This is a vain pretension;
Go, remove yourself from me, O vain pretender,
Or proceed to give proofs and evidence
That this is generic water, and concrete water thereof'?
Or when a mother cries to her sucking babe,
'Come, O son, I am thy mother,'

Does the babe answer, 'O mother, show a proof
That I shall find comfort from taking thy milk'?
In the hearts of every sect that has a taste of the truth
The sight and the voice of prophets work miracles.
When the prophets raise their cry to the outward ear,
The souls of each sect bow in devotion within;
Because never in this world hath the soul's ear
Heard from any man the like of that cry.

*Masnavi— Book 2: 16*

## Tree Of Knowledge

This is the tree of knowledge, O knowing one;
Very high, very fine, very expansive,
The very water of life from the circumfluent ocean.
Thou hast run after form, O ill-informed one,
Wherefore thou lackest the fruit of the tree of substance.
Sometimes it is named tree, sometimes sun,
Sometimes lake, and sometimes cloud.
'Tis one, though it has thousands of manifestations;
Its least manifestation is eternal life!
Though 'tis one, it has a thousand manifestations,
The names that fit that one are countless.
That one is to thy personality a father,
In regard to another person He may be a son.
In relation to another He may be wrath and vengeance,
In relation to another, mercy and goodness.
He has thousands of names, yet is One,
Answering to all of His descriptions, yet indescribable.
Every one who seeks names, if he is a man of credulity,
Like thee, remains hopeless and frustrated of his aim.
Why cleavest thou to this mere name of tree,
So that thou art utterly balked and disappointed?
Pass over names and look to qualities,
So that qualities may lead thee to essence!
The differences of sects arise from His names;
When they pierce to His essence they find His peace!"

*Masnavi— Book 2: 17*

# Ducks

The Young Ducks who were brought up under a Hen.
Although a domestic fowl may have taken thee,
Who art a duckling, under her wing and nurtured thee,
Thy mother was a duck of that ocean.
Thy nurse was earthy, and her wing dry land.
The longing for the ocean which fills thy heart,
That natural longing of thy soul comes from thy mother.
Thy longing for dry land comes to thee from thy nurse;
Quit thy nurse, for she will lead thee astray.
Leave thy nurse on the dry land and push on,
Enter the ocean of real Being, like the ducks!
Though thy nurse may frighten thee away from water,
Do thou fear not, but haste on into the ocean!
Thou art a duck, and flourishest on land and water,
And dost not, like a domestic fowl, dig up the house.

*Masnavi— Book 2: 18*

## The Smell Of Evil Deeds

Evil deeds give men's prayers an ill savour in God's nostrils.
Thou art asleep, and the smell of that forbidden fruit
Ascends to the azure skies,
Ascends along with thy foul breath,
Till it overpowers heaven with stench;
Stench of pride, stench of lust, stench of greed.
All these stink like onions when a man speaks.
Though thou swearest, saying, "When have I eaten?
Have I not abstained from onions and garlic?"
The very breath of that oath tells tales,
As it strikes the nostrils of them that sit with thee.

*Masnavi— Book 3: 1*

## From Reason And Mind

Just so an ant who saw a pen writing on paper,
Delivered himself to another ant in this way
'That pen is making very wonderful figures,
Like hyacinths and lilies and roses.'
The other said, 'The finger is the real worker,
The pen is only the instrument of its working.'
A third ant said, 'No; the action proceeds from the arm,
The weak finger writes with the arm's might.'
So it went on upwards, till at last
A prince of the ants, who had some wit
Said, 'Ye regard only the outward form of this marvel,
Which form becomes senseless in sleep and death.
Form is only as a dress or a staff in the hand,
It is only from reason and mind these figures proceed.'

*Masnavi— Book 4: 9*

## The Seeker

The monk said, "I am searching everywhere for a man
Who lives by the life of the breath of God."
The other said, "Here are men; the bazaar is full;
These are surely men, O enlightened sage!"
The monk said, "I seek a man who walks straight
As well in the road of anger as in that of lust.
Where is one who shows himself a man in anger and lust?
In search of such a one I run from street to street.
If there be one who is a true man in these two states,
I will yield up my life for him this day!"
The other, who was a fatalist, said, "What you seek is rare.
But you are ignorant of the force of the divine decree;
You see the branches, but ignore the root.
We men are but branches, God's eternal decree the root.
That decree turns from its course the revolving sky,
And makes foolish hundreds of planets like Mercury.
It reduces to helplessness the world of devices;
It turns steel and stone to water.
O you who attribute stability to these steps on the road,
You are one of the raw ones; yea, raw, raw!
When you have seen the millstone turning round,
Then, prithee, go and see the stream that turns it.
When you have seen the dust rising up into the air,
Go and mark the air in the midst of the dust.
You see the kettles of thought boiling over,
Look with intelligence at the fire beneath them.

God said to Job, 'Out of my clemency
I have given a grain of patience to every hair of thine.'
Look not, then, so much at your own patience;
After seeing patience, look to the Giver of patience.
How long will you confine your view to the waterwheel?
Lift up your head and view also the water."

*Masnavi— Book 5: 10*

## Evil Doubts, Evil Friends

Since thou hast been led astray by faithless men,
Turn now from thy evil doubts to the opposite mind.
I am free from error and all faithlessness;
Thou must come to me and rescind evil doubts.
Cut off these evil doubts and cast them away,
For in the presence of such thou becomest double.
Therefore thou hast chosen harsh friends and companions;
If I ask where they are thou sayest they are gone.
The good friend goes up to highest heaven,
Evil friends sink beneath the bottom of the earth,
Whilst thou art left alone in the midst, forlorn,
Even as the fires left by the departed caravan.

*Masnavi— Book 3: 2*

## My Companions, The Stars

The Prophet said, "My companions are as the stars,
Lights to them that walk aright, missiles against Satan.
If every man had strength of eyesight
To look straight at the light of the sun in heaven,
What need were there of stars, O humble one,
To one who was guided by the light of the sun?
Neither moon nor planets would be needed
By one who saw directly the Sun of 'The Truth.'
The Moon declares, as also the clouds and shadows,
'I am a man, yet it hath been revealed to me.'
Like you, I was naturally dark,
'Twas the Sun's revelation that gave me such light.
I still am dark compared to the Sun,
Though I am light compared to the dark souls of men.
Therefore is my light weak, that you may bear it,
For you are not strong enough to bear the dazzling Sun.
I have, as it were, mixed honey with vinegar,
To succour the sickness of your hearts.
When you are cured of your sickness, O invalid,
Then leave out the vinegar and eat pure honey.
When the heart is garnished and swept clear of lust,
Therein 'The God of Mercy sitteth on His throne.'
Then God rules the heart immediately,
When it has gained this immediate connection with Him.

*Masnavi*— Book 1: 15

# The Snake

Lust is that snake; How say you, it is dead?
It is only frozen by the pangs of hunger.
If it obtains the state of Pharaoh,
So as to command the (frozen) rivers to flow,
Straightway it is led to pride like Pharaoh's,
And it plunders the goods of many a Moses and Aaron.
Through pressure of want this snake is as a fly,
It becomes a gnat through wealth and rank and luxury.
Beware, keep that snake in the frost of humiliation,
Draw it not forth into the sunshine of 'Iraq!
So long as that snake is frozen, it is well;
When it finds release from frost you become its prey.
Conquer it and save yourself from being conquered,
Pity it not, it is not one who bears affection.
For that warmth of the sun kindles its lust,
And that bat of vileness flaps its wings.
Slay it in sacred war and combat,
Like a valiant man will God requite you with union.
When that man cherished that snake,
That stubborn brute was happy in the luxury of warmth;
And of necessity worked destruction, O friend;
Yea, many more mischiefs than I have told.
If you wish to keep that snake tied up
Without trouble, be faithful, be faithful!
But how can base men attain this wish?
It requires a Moses to slay serpents;

And a hundred thousand men were slain by his serpent,
In dire confusion, according to his purpose.

*Masnavi— Book 3: 4*

## Lost In The Evil Spirit

When a man is possessed by an evil spirit
The qualities of humanity are lost in him.
Whatever he says is really said by that spirit,
Though it seems to proceed from the man's mouth.
When the spirit has this rule and dominance over him,
The agent is the property of the spirit, and not himself;
His self is departed, and he has become the spirit.

*Masnavi— Book 4: 4*

## From One Danger To A Worse

What is more lovely than committing oneself to God?
Many there are who flee from one danger to a worse;
Many flee from a snake and meet a dragon.
Man plans a stratagem, and thereby snares himself;
What he takes for life turns out, to be destruction.
He shuts the door after his foe is in the house.

*Masnavi*— Book 1: 5

# Infidelity

"The Prophet, whose words are as a seal,
Said, 'Acquiescence in infidelity is infidelity.'
And again, 'Acquiescence in God's ordinance
Is incumbent on all true believers.'
Infidelity and hypocrisy are not ordained of God;
If I acquiesce in them I am at variance with God.
And yet, if I acquiesce not, that again is wrong;
What way of escape is there from this dilemma? "
I said to him, "This infidelity is ordained, not ordinance,
Though this infidelity is the work of the ordinance.
Therefore distinguish the ordinance from the ordained,
That thy difficulty may be at once removed.
I acquiesce in infidelity so far as it is God's ordinance,
Not so far as it is our evil and foul passions.
Infidelity qua ordinance is not infidelity,
Call not God an infidel. Set not foot in this place.
Infidelity is folly, ordained infidelity wisdom,
How can mercy and vengeance be the same?
Ugliness of the picture is not ugliness of the painter,
Not so, for he erases ugly pictures.
The ability of the painter is shown in this,
That he can paint both ugly and beautiful pictures.
If I should pursue this argument properly,
So that questions and answers should be prolonged,
The unction of the mystery of love would escape me,
The picture of obedience would become another picture."

*Masnavi— Book 3: 5*

# Black And White

A certain man whose hair was half gray came in haste
To a barber who was a friend of his,
Saying, "Pluck out the white hairs from my beard,
For I have selected a young bride, O my son.
The barber cut off his beard and laid it before him,
Saying, "Do you part them, the task is beyond me."
Questions are white and answers black; do you choose,
For the man of faith knows not how to choose.

*Masnavi— Book 3: 5*

## Abstinence

Abstinence is the prince of medicines,
As scratching only aggravates a scab.
Abstinence is certainly the root of medicine;
Practise abstinence, see how it invigorates thy soul!
Accept this counsel and give ear thereto,
That it may be to thee as an earring of gold!
Nay, not a mere earring, but that thou mayest be a mine of gold,
Or that thou mayest surpass moon and Pleiades.

*Masnavi— Book 1: 9*

# 'Tis I

Once a man came and knocked at the door of his friend.
His friend said, "who art thou. O faithful one?"
He said, "'Tis I." He answered, "There is no admittance.
There is no room for the 'raw' at my well-cooked feast.
Naught but fire of separation and absence
Can cook the raw one and free him from hypocrisy!
Since thy 'self' has not yet left thee,
Thou must be burned in fiery flames."
The poor man went away, and for one whole year
Journeyed burning with grief for his friend's absence.
His heart burned till it was cooked; then he went again
And drew near to the house of his friend.
He knocked at the door in fear and trepidation
Lest some careless word might fall from his lips.
His friend shouted, "Who is that at the door?"
He answered, "'Tis Thou who art at the door. O Beloved!"
The friend said, "Since 'tis I, let me come in,
There is not room for two 'I's' in one house."

*Masnavi— Book 1: 11*

# Regrets

The dead regret not dying, but having lost opportunities in life.
Well said that Leader of mankind,
That whosoever passes away from the world
Does not grieve and lament over his death,
But grieves ever over lost opportunities.
He says, "Why did I not keep death always in view,
Which is the treasury of wealth and sustenance?
Why did I blindly all my life set my affections
On vain shadows which perish at death?
My regret is not that I have died,
But that I rested on these vain shadows in life."

*Masnavi— Book 6: 5*

## No Chain Binds Him

Behold that king's son clad in rags,
With bare head and fallen into distress;
Consumed by lusts and riotous living,
Having sold all his clothes and substance;
Having lost house and home, utterly disgraced,
Fulfilling the desire of his enemies by his disgrace.
If he sees a pious man he cries, "O sir,
Aid me, for the love of God;
For I have fallen into this dire disgrace;
I have squandered goods and gold and wealth.
Aid me so that perchance I may escape hence,
And extricate myself from this deep slough."
He repeats this prayer to high and low,
"Release me, release me, release me!"
His eyes and ears are open, and he is free from bonds,
No jailer watches him, no chain binds him;
What, then, is the bond from which he asks release?
What is the prison from which ho seeks an exit?
'Tis the bond of God's purpose and hidden decrees;
Ah! none but the pure in sight can see that bond;
Though not visible, that bond exists in concealment;
'Tis more stringent than prison or chains of iron,
For the mason can pull down prison walls,
And blacksmiths can break asunder iron chains;
But, strange to say, this ponderous hidden bond,
Blacksmiths are impotent to break this asunder!

*Masnavi— Book 3: 9*

## The Garden Knows

If his thorn puts not forth a single rosebud,
The spring in disclosing him is his foe.
But he who is from head to foot a perfect rose or lily,
To him spring brings rejoicing.
The useless thorn desires the autumn,
That autumn may associate itself with the garden;
And hide the rose's beauty and the thorn's shame,
That men may not see the bloom of the one and the other's shame,
That common stone and pure ruby may appear all as one.
True, the Gardener knows the difference even in autumn,
But the sight of One is better than the world's sight.
That One Person is Himself the world, as He is the sun,
And every star in heaven is a part of the sun.
That One Person is Himself the world, and the rest
Are all His dependents and parasites, O man!
He is the perfect world, yet He is single;
He holds in hand the writing of the whole of existence.
Wherefore all forms and colours of beauty cry out,
"Good news! good news! Lo! the spring is at hand!"
If the blossoms did not shine as bright helmets,
How could the fruits display their globes?
When the blossoms are shed the fruits come to a head,
When tho body is destroyed the soul lifts up its head.
The fruit is the substance, the blossom only its form,
Blossom the good news, and fruit the promised boon.

When the blossoms fall the fruit appears,
When the former vanish the fruit is tasted.
Till bread is broken, how can it serve as food?
Till the grapes are crushed, how can they yield wine?
Till citrons be pounded up with drugs,
How can they afford healing to the sick?

*Masnavi— Book 1: 9*

## Weeds On Water

Sensations and thoughts resemble weeds
Which occupy the surface of pure water.
The hand of reason puts these weeds aside,
And the pure water is then visible to the wise.
Weeds in plenty cover the stream like bubbles;
When they are swept aside, the water is seen;
But when God unlooses not the hands of reason,
The weeds on our water grow thick through carnal lust;
Yea, they cover up your water more and more,
While your lust is smiling and your reason weeping.

*Masnavi— Book 3: 10*

# I Know Not

I know not if thou art a moon or an idol,
I know not what thou requirest of me.
I know not what service to pay thee,
Whether to keep silence or to speak.
Thou art not apart from me, yet, strange to say,
I know not where I am, or where thou art.
I know not wherefore thou art dragging me,
Now embracing me, and now wounding me!

*Masnavi— Book 6: 3*

## Tear Not Thy Plumage Off

Tear not thy plumage off it cannot be replaced;
Disfigure not thy face in wantonness, O fair one!
That face which is bright as the forenoon sun,
To disfigure it were a grievous sin.
'Twere paganism to mar such a face as thine!
The moon itself would weep to lose sight of it!
Knowest thou not the beauty of thine own face?
Quit this temper that leads thee to war with thyself!
It is the claws of thine own foolish thoughts
That in spite wound the face of thy quiet soul.
Know such thoughts to be claws fraught with poison,
Which score deep wounds on the face of thy soul.
Rend not thy plumage off, but avert thy heart from it
For hostility between them is the law of this holy war.
Were there no hostility, that war would be impossible.

*Masnavi— Book 5: 3*

# One Religion

All religions are in substance one and the same.
In the adorations and benedictions of righteous men
The praises of all the prophets are kneaded together.
All their praises are mingled into one stream,
All the vessels are emptied into one ewer.
Because He that is praised is, in fact, only One,
In this respect all religions are only one religion.

*Masnavi— Book 3: 12*

## God The Creator

God is the creator of heaven and them that dwell therein;
Also of water and of earth, and them that dwell therein;
To heaven He gave its revolutions and its purity,
To the earth its dark look and appearance.
Can the heaven will to become as dregs?
Can earth will to assume the clearness of pure wine?
That Person has assigned 'to each its lot,
Can mountain by endeavour become as grass?'
The prophets answered, "Verily God has created
Some qualities in you which you cannot alter;
But He has created other accidental qualities,
Which, being objectionable, may be made good.
Bid stone become gold that is impossible;
Bid copper become gold that is possible.
Bid sand bloom as a rose it cannot;
Bid dust turn to mud that is within its capacity.
God has sent some pains for which there is no cure,
Such, for instance, as lameness, loss of nose, and blindness.
God has sent other pains for which there are cures,
To wit, crooked mouth and headache.
God has ordained these remedies of His mercy;
The use of these in pain and anguish is not in vain."

*Masnavi— Book 3: 13*

# Awakening

The people of the world lie unconscious,
With veils drawn over their faces, and asleep;
But when the morn shall burst forth and the sun arise
Every creature will raise its head from its couch;
To the unconscious God will restore consciousness;
They will stand in rings as slaves with rings in ears;
Dancing and clapping hands with songs of praise,
Singing with joy, "Our Lord hath restored us to life!"
Shedding their old skins and bones,
As horsemen stirring up a cloud of dust.
All pressing on from Not-being to Being,
On the last day, as well the thankful as the unthankful.

*Masnavi*— Book 1: 15

## Release From Danger

Suppose you are sleeping in a place of danger,
And serpents are drawing near to bite your head,
A kind friend will inform you of your danger,
Saying, 'Jump up, lest the serpent devour you.'
You reply, 'Why do you utter evil presages?'
He answers, 'What presage? Up, and see for yourself!
By means of this evil presage I rouse you,
And release you from danger and lead you to your home.'
Like a prophet he warns you of hidden danger,
For a prophet sees what worldlings cannot see.

*Masnavi— Book 3: 13*

# Right Uses

Though the object of a book is to teach an art,
If you make a pillow of it, it serves that purpose too.
Yet its main object is not to serve as a pillow,
But to impart knowledge and useful instruction.
If you use a sword for a tent-peg,
You prefer the worse use of it to the better.
Though the object of all men's being is wisdom,
Yet each man has a different place of worship.
The place of worship of the noble is nobility,
The place of worship of the base is degradation.

*Masnavi— Book 3: 13*

## Soul's Awakening

Sleep of the body the soul's awakening.
Every night Thou freest our spirits from the body
And its snare, making them pure as rased tablets.
Every night spirits are released from this cage,
And set free, neither lording it nor lorded over.
At night prisoners are unaware of their prison,
At night kings are unaware of their majesty.
Then there is no thought or care for loss or gain,
No regard to such an one or such an one.
The state of the "Knower" is such as this, even when awake.
God says, "Thou wouldst deem him awake though asleep,
Sleeping to the affairs of the world, day and night,
Like a pen in the directing hand of the writer.
He who sees not the hand which effects the writing
Fancies the effect proceeds from the motion of the pen.
If the "Knower" revealed the particulars of this state,
'Twould rob the vulgar of their sensual sleep.
His soul wanders in the desert that has no similitude;
Like his body, his spirit is enjoying perfect rest;
Freed from desire of eating and drinking,
Like a bird escaped from cage and snare.

*Masnavi— Book 1: 3*

# Sleepers

The more a man is awake, the more he sleeps;
His wakefulness is worse than slumbering.
Our wakefulness fetters our spirits,
Then our souls are a prey to divers whims,
Thoughts of loss and gain and fears of misery.
They retain not purity, nor dignity, nor lustre,
Nor aspiration to soar heavenwards.
That one is really sleeping who hankers after each whim
And holds parley with each fancy.

*Masnavi— Book 1: 3*

## Banishing Fears

When the merchant goes to his shop in the morning,
He does so in hope and probability of gaining bread.
If you have no hope of getting bread, why go?
There is the fear of loss, since you are not strong.
But does not this fear of utter loss in your trade
Become weakened in the course of your exertions?
You say, "Although the fear of loss is before me,
Yet I feel greater fear in remaining idle.
I have a better hope through exerting myself;
My fear is increased by remaining idle."

*Masnavi— Book 3: 13*

## Tree Of Man

The heart of man is like the root of a tree,
Therefrom grow the leaves on firm branches.
Corresponding to that root grow up branches
As well on the tree as on souls and intellects.
The tops of the perfect trees reach the heavens,
The roots firm, and the branches in the sky.
Since then the tree of love has grown up to heaven,
How shall it not also grow in the heart of the Prince?

*Masnavi— Book 3: 17*

## Taught Be God

If ye really have trust in God, exert yourselves,
And strive, in constant reliance on the Almighty.
Wisdom is granted often times to the weak.
He said, "O friends, God has given me inspiration.
Often times strong counsel is suggested to the weak.
The wit taught by God to the bee
Is withheld from the lion and the wild ass.
It fills its cells with liquid sweets,
For God opens the door of this knowledge to it.
The skill taught by God to the silkworm
Is a learning beyond the reach of the elephant.

*Masnavi— Book 1: 5*

## Secret Sins

Thy secret sins are manifest; no divulging is needed.
There is no need to proclaim thy sins,
All men are cognisant of thy sin-burnt heart.
Thy soul every moment casts up sparks of fire,
Which say, "See me a man destined to the fire;
I am a part of the fire, and go to join my whole;
Not a light, so that I should join the Source of light."

*Masnavi— Book 3: 12*

## Colours And Light

Outward colours arise from the light of sun and stars,
And inward colours from the Light on high.
The light that lights the eye is also the heart's Light;
The eye's light proceeds from the Light of the heart.

*Masnavi— Book 1: 5*

## Potherbs

Behold these potherbs boiling in the pot,
How they jump and toss about in the heat of the fire.
Whilst they are boiling, they keep leaping up,
Even to the top of the pot, and utter cries,
Saying to the housewife, "Why do you set us on the fire?
Now you have bought us, why should you afflict us?"
The housewife pushes them down with her spoon, saying,
"Be still, and boil well, and leap not off the fire.
I do not boil you because I dislike you,
But that you may acquire a good savour and taste.
When you become food you will be mingled with life;
This trial is not imposed on you to distress you.
In the garden you drank water soft and fresh;
That water-fed one was reserved for this fire.
Mercy was first shown to it before vengeance,
That mercy might train it to be proof against trial;
Mercy was shown to it previously to vengeance,
That it might acquire its substance of being.
Because flesh and skin grow not without tender care,
How should they not grow when warmed by the Friend's love.
If vengeance follows as a necessary consequence,
That you may make an offering of that substance,
Mercy follows again to compensate for it,
That you may be purified and raised above your nature."

*Masnavi— Book 3: 18*

## Painting On A Wall

A painting on a wall resembles a man,
But see what it is lacking in that empty form.
'Tis life that is lacking to that mere semblance of man.

*Masnavi—Book 1: 5*

## The Work Of Each

The heaven is busily toiling through ages,
Just as men labour to provide food for women.
And the earth does the woman's work, and toils
In bearing offspring and suckling them.
Know then earth and heaven are endued with sense,
Since they act like persons endued with sense.
If these two lovers did not suck nutriment from each other,
Why should they creep together like man and wife?
Without the earth how could roses and saffron grow?
For naught can grow from the sole heat and rain of heaven.
This is the cause of the female seeking the male,
That the work of each may be accomplished.

*Masnavi— Book 3: 17*

## God Speaks

God speaks words of power to souls,
To things of naught, without eyes or ears,
And at these words they all spring into motion;
At His words of power these nothings arise quickly,
And strong impulse urges them into existence.
Again, He speaks other spells to these creatures,
And swiftly drives them back again into Not-being.
He speaks to the rose's ear, and causes it to bloom;
He speaks to the tulip, and makes it blossom.
He speaks a spell to body, and it becomes soul;
He speaks to the sun, and it becomes a fount of light.
Again, in its ear He whispers a word of power,
And its face is darkened as by a hundred eclipses.
What is it that God says to the ear of earth,
That it attends thereto and rests steadfast?
What is it that Speaker says to the cloud,
That it pours forth rain-water like a water-skin?
Whosoever is bewildered by wavering will,
In his ear hath God whispered His riddle,
That He may bind him on the horns of a dilemma;
For he says, 'Shall I do this or its reverse?'
Also from God comes the preference of one alternative;
'Tis from God's impulsion that man chooses one of the two.
If you desire sanity in this embarrassment,
Stuff not the ear of your mind with cotton.
Take the cotton of evil suggestions from the mind's ear,

That the heavenly voice from above may enter it,
That you may understand that riddle of His,
That you may be cognisant of that open secret.

*Masnavi— Book 1: 6*

# Reasons

What worlds the principle of Reason embraces!
How broad is this ocean of Reason!
Yea, the Reason of man is a boundless ocean.
O son, that ocean requires, as it were, a diver.
On this fair ocean our human forms
Float about, like bowls on the surface of water;
Yea like cups on the surface, till they are. filled;
And when filled, these cups sink into the water.
The ocean of Reason is not seen ; reasoning men are seen;
But our forms (minds) are only as waves or spray thereof.
Whatever form that ocean uses as its instrument,
Therewith it casts its spray far and wide.

*Masnavi— Book 1: 5*

## Sent From Heaven

Heaven is man and earth woman in character;
Whatever heaven sends it, earth cherishes.
When earth lacks heat, heaven sends heat;
When it lacks moisture and dew, heaven sends them.
The earthy sign 9 succours the terrestrial earth,
The watery sign (Aquarius) sends moisture to it;
The windy sign sends the clouds to it,
To draw off unwholesome exhalations.
The fiery sign (Leo) sends forth the heat of the sun,
Like a dish heated red-hot in front and behind.

*Masnavi— Book 3: 17*

## The Prophet Said...

The Prophet said, 'Mine eyes sleep,
But my heart is awake with the Lord of mankind.'
Your eyes are awake and your heart fast asleep,
My eyes are closed, and my heart at the 'open door.'
My heart has other five senses of its own;
These senses of my heart view the two worlds.
Let not a weakling like you censure me,
What, seems night to you is broad day to me;
What seems a prison to you is a garden to me.
Busiest occupation is rest to me.
Your feet are in the mire, to me, mire is rose,
What to you is funeral wailing is marriage drum to me.
While I seem on earth, abiding with you in the house,
I ascend like Saturn to the seventh heaven.
'Tis not I who companion with you, 'tis my shadow;
My exaltation transcends your thoughts,
Because I have transcended thought,
Yea, I have sped beyond reach of thought.
I am lord of thought, not overlorded by thought,
As the builder is lord of the building.
All creatures are enslaved to thought;
For this cause are they sad at heart and sorrowful.
I send myself on an embassy to thought,
And, at will, spring back again from thought.

*Masnavi*— Book 2: 16

## No Absolutes

In the world there is nothing absolutely bad;
Know, moreover, evil is only relative.
In the world there is neither poison nor antidote,
Which is not a foot to one and a fetter to another;
To one the power of moving, to another a clog;
To one a poison, to another an antidote.
Serpents' poison is life to serpents,
In relation to mankind it is death.
To the creatures of the sea the sea is a garden,
To the creatures of the land it is fatal.
In the same way, O man, reckon up with intelligence
The relations of these things in endless variety.

*Masnavi— Book 4: 1*

# Love

Love is a perfect muzzle of evil suggestions;
Without love who ever succeeded in stopping them?
Be a lover, and seek that fair Beauty,
Hunt for that Waterfowl in every stream!
How can you get water from that which cuts it off?
How gain understanding from what destroys understanding?

*Masnavi— book 5: 11*

## The Spheres' Song

Philosophers say that we have learned
Our melodies from those of the revolving spheres.
The song of the spheres in their revolutions
Is what men sing with lute and voice.
The faithful hold that the sweet influences of heaven
Can make even harsh voices melodious.

*Masnavi— Book 4: 2*

## Fearless Love

The sect of lovers is distinct from all others,
Lovers have a religion and a faith of their own.
Though the ruby has no stamp, what matters it?
Love is fearless in the midst of the sea of fear.

*Masnavai*— Book 2: 7

# Black Coal

Thy lust is even as fire burning in thy evil deeds;
The black coal of these deeds is lighted by the fire;
The blackness of the coal is first hidden by the fire,
But, when it is burnt, the blackness is made visible.

*Masnavi— Book 4: 2*

## Bad Friends

When the body bows in worship, the heart is a temple,
And where there is a temple, there bad friends are weeds
When a liking for bad friends grows up in you,
Flee from them, and avoid converse with them.
Root up those weeds, for, if they attain full growth,
They will subvert you and your temple together.
O beloved, this weed is deviation from the "right way,"
You crawl crookedly, like infants unable to walk.
Fear not to acknowledge your ignorance and guilt,
That the Heavenly Master may not withhold instruction.
When you say, "I am ignorant; O teach me,"
Such open confession is better than false pride.

*Masnavi— Book 4: 2*

## Journeying

"I journeyed long time to East and to West,
I journeyed years and months for love of that Moon,
Heedless of the way, absorbed in God.
With bare feet I trod upon thorns and flints,
Seeing I was bewildered, and beside myself, and senseless.
Think not my feet touched the earth,
For the lover verily travels with the heart.
What knows the heart of road and stages?
What of distant and near, while it is drunk with love?
Distance and nearness are attributes of bodies,
The journeys of spirits are after another sort.
You journeyed from the embryo state to rationality
Without footsteps or stages or change of place,
The journey of the soul involves not time and place.
And my body learnt from the soul its mode of journeying,
Now my body has renounced the bodily mode of journeying;
It journeys secretly and without form, though under a form."

*Masnavi— Book 3: 12*

# The Thirst And The Water

The man athirst cries, "Where is delicious water?"
Water too cries, "Where is the water-drinker?"
This thirst in my soul is the attraction of the water;
I am the water's and the water is mine.
God's wisdom in His eternal foreknowledge and decree
Made us to be lovers one of the other.

*Masnavi— Book 3: 17*

## Battling Against Advice

How were you compelled to sin when you took such pleasure
And pride in engaging in those sins?
Does a man feel such pleasure in acting on compulsion
As he exhibits when committing wrong actions?
You battle like twenty men against those
Who give you good advice not to do that act;
Saying to them, "This is right and quite proper;
Who dissuades me from it but men of no account?"
Does a man acting on compulsion talk like this?
Or rather one who is erring of his own freewill?
Whatever your lust wills you deem freewill,
What reason demands you deem compulsion.

*Masnavi— Book 4: 2*

*Rumi*

## The Tree Is Born From The Fruit

Seemingly the bough is the cause of the fruit,
But really the bough exists because of the fruit.
Were he not impelled by desire of fruit,
The gardener would never have planted the tree.
Therefore in reality the tree is born from the fruit,
Though seemingly the fruit is born from the tree.

*Masnavi*— Book 4: 2

# The Love Of The soul

The body loves green pastures and running water,
For this cause that its origin is from them.
The love of the soul is for life and the living one,
Because its origin is the Soul not bound to place.
The love of the soul is for wisdom and knowledge,
That of the body for houses, gardens, and vineyards;
The love of the soul is for things exalted on high,
That of the body for acquisition of goods and food.

*Masnavi— Book 3: 17*

# Chains

Men are as demons, and lust of wealth their chain,
Which drags them forth to toil in shop and field.
This chain is made of their fears and anxieties.
Deem not that these men have no chain upon them.
It causes them to engage in labour and the chase,
It forces them to toil in mines and on the sea,
It urges them towards good and towards evil.

*Masnavi— Book 4: 2*

## God's Servants

Air, earth, water, and fire are God's servants.
To us they seem lifeless, but to God living.
In God's presence fire ever waits to do its service,
Like a submissive lover with no will of its own.
When you strike steel on flint fire leaps forth;
But 'tis by God's command it thus steps forth.
Strike not together the flint and steel of wrong,
For the pair will generate more, like man and woman.

Though water be enclosed in a reservoir,
Yet air will absorb it, for 'tis its supporter;
It sets it free and bears it to its source,
Little by little, so that you see not the process.
In like manner this breath of ours by degrees
Steals away our souls from the prison-house of earth.

*Masnavi— Book 1: 4*

## Sight Restored

He who has emerged from the veil of blind belief
Beholds by the light of God all things that exist.
His pure light, without signs or tokens,
Cleaves for him the rind and brings him to the kernel.

*Masnavi—Book 4: 4*

## Hidden Treasure

The people of this world exist in order to manifest
And to disclose the 'hidden treasure.'
Read, "I was a hidden treasure, and desired to be known;
Hide not the hidden treasure, but disclose it.
Your true treasure is hidden under a false one,
Just as butter is hidden within the substance of milk.
The false one is this transitory body of yours,
The true one your divine soul.
Long time this milk is exposed to view,
And the soul's butter is hidden and of no account.
Stir up your milk assiduously with knowledge,
So that what is hidden in it may be disclosed;
Because this mortal is the guide to immortality,
As the cries of revellers indicate the cup-bearer."

*Masnavi— Book 4: 7*

## The Tree Counsels

A man captured a bird by wiles and snares;
The bird said to him, "O noble sir,
In your time you have eaten many oxen and sheep,
And likewise sacrificed many camels;
You have never become satisfied with their meat,
So you will not be satisfied with my flesh.
Let me go, that I may give you three counsels,
Whence you will see whether I am wise or foolish.
The first of my counsels shall be given on your wrist,
The second on your well-plastered roof,
And the third I will give you from the top of a tree.
On hearing all three you will deem yourself happy.
As regards the counsel on your wrist, 'tis this.
'Believe not foolish assertions of any one!'"
When he had spoken this counsel on his wrist, he flew
Up to the top of the roof, entirely free.
Then he said, "Do not grieve for what is past;
When a thing is done, vex not yourself about it."
He continued, "Hidden inside this body of mine
Is a precious pearl, ten drachms in weight.
That jewel of right, belonged to you,
Wealth for yourself and prosperity for your children.
You have lost it, as it, was not fated you should get it,
That pearl whose like can nowhere be found."
Thereupon the man, like a woman in her travail,
Gave vent to lamentations and weeping.

The bird said to him, "Did I not counsel you, saying,
'Beware of grieving over what is past and gone?'
When 'tis past and gone, why sorrow for it?
Either you understood not my counsel or are deaf.
The second counsel I gave you was this, namely,
'Be not misguided enough to believe foolish assertions.'
O fool, altogether I do not weigh three drachms,
How can a pearl of ten drachms be within me?"
The man recovered himself and said, "Well then,
Tell me now your third good counsel!"
The bird replied, "You have made a fine use of the others,
That I should waste my third counsel upon you.
To give counsel to a sleepy ignoramus
Is to sow seeds upon salt land.
Torn garments of folly and ignorance cannot be patched.
O counsellors, waste not the seed of counsel on them!"

*Masnavi— Book 4: 5*

# The World Is Transitory

Last night a Sunni said, "The world is transitory;
The heavens will pass away; 'God will be the heir.'"
A philosopher replied, "How know you they are transitory?
How knows the rain the transitory nature of the cloud?
Are you not a mere mote floating in the sunbeams?
How know you that the sun is transitory?
A mere worm buried in a dung-heap,
How can it know the origin and end of the earth?
In blind belief you have accepted this from your father,
And through folly have clung to it ever since.
Tell me what is the proof of its transitoriness,
Or else be silent and indulge not in idle talk."
The Sunni said, "One day I saw two persons
Engaged in argument on this deep question,
Yea, in dispute and controversy and argument.
At last a crowd was gathered round them.
I proceeded towards that company
To inform myself of the subject of their discourse.
One said, 'This sky will pass away;
Doubtless this building had a builder.'
The other said, 'It is eternal and without period;
It had no builder, or it was its own builder.'
The first said, 'Do you then deny the Creator,
The Bringer of day and night, the Sustainer of men?'
He answered, 'Without proof I will not listen
To what you say; 'tis only based on blind belief.

Go! bring proof and evidence, for never
Will I accept this statement without proof.'
He answered, 'The proof is within my heart,
Yea, my proofs are hidden in my heart.
From weakness of vision you see not the new moon;
If I see it, be not angry with me!'
...Then the first said, 'O friend, within me is a proof
Which assures me of the transitoriness of the heavens.
I hold it for certain, and the sign of certainty
In him who possesses it is entering into fire.
Know this proof is not to be expressed in speech,
Any more than the feeling of love felt by lovers.
When the tears course down my cheeks,
They are a proof of the beauty and grace of my beloved.'
The other said, 'I take not these for a proof,
Though they may be a proof to common people.'"
The Sunni said, "When genuine and base coin boast,
Saying, 'Thou art false, I am good and genuine,'
Fire is the test ultimately,
When the two rivals are cast into the furnace."
Accordingly both of them entered the furnace,
Both leapt into the fiery flame;
And the philosopher was burnt to ashes,
But the God-fearing Sunni was made fairer than before.

*Masnavi— Book 6: 4*

## True Reason

Cleverness is like Canaan's swimming in the ocean;
'Tis no river or small stream; 'tis the mighty ocean.
Away with this attempt to swim; quit self-conceit.
'Twill not save you; Canaan was drowned at last.
Love is as the ark appointed for the righteous,
Which annuls the danger and provides a way of escape.
Sell your cleverness and buy bewilderment;
Cleverness is mere opinion, bewilderment intuition.
Make sacrifice of your reason at the feet of Mustafa,
Say, "God Sufficeth me, for He, is sufficient for me."
Do not, like Canaan, hang back from entering the ark,
Being puffed up with vain conceit of cleverness.
He said, "I will escape to the top of high mountains,
Why need I put myself under obligation to Noah?"
Ah! better for him had he never learnt swimming!
Then he would have based his hopes on Noah's ark.
Would he had been ignorant of craft as a babe!
Then like a babe he would have clung to his mother.
Would he had been less full of borrowed knowledge!
Then he would have accepted inspired knowledge from his father.
When, with inspiration at hand, you seek book-learning,
Your heart, as if inspired, loads you with reproach.
Traditional knowledge, when inspiration is available,
Is like making ablutions with sand when water is near.
Make yourself ignorant, be submissive, and then

You will obtain release from your ignorance.
For this cause, O son, the Prince of men declared,
"The majority of those in Paradise are the foolish."
Cleverness is as a wind raising storms of pride;
Be foolish, so that your heart may be at peace;
Not with the folly that doubles itself by vain babble,
But with that arising from bewilderment at "The Truth."
Those Egyptian women who cut their hands were fools
Fools as to their hands, being amazed at Yusuf's face.
Make sacrifice of reason to love of "The Friend,"
True reason is to be found where He is.
Men of wisdom direct their reason heavenwards,
Vain babblers halt on earth where no "Friend" is.
If through bewilderment your reason quits your head,
Every hair of your head becomes true reason and a head.

*Masnavi— Book 4: 2*

## Food For The Soul

The right road is attainable,
For the heart's life is the food of the soul.
Whatever is enjoyed by the carnal man
Yields no fruit, even as salt and waste land.
Its result is naught but remorse,
Its traffic yields only loss.
It is not profitable in the long run;
Its name is called 'bankrupt' in the upshot.
Discern, then, the bankrupt from the profitable,
Consider the eventual value of this and that.

*Masnavi— Book 1: 3*

## To The Birds

Souls are disgraced by union with bodies,
Bodies are ennobled by union with souls.
Arise, O lovers; this sweet draught is yours;
Ye are they that endure; eternal life is yours.
Ho! ye that seek, arise and take your fill of love,
Snuff up that perfume of Yusuf!
Approach, O Solomon, thou that knowest birds' language,
Sound the note of every bird that draws near;
When God sent, thee to the birds,
He taught thee first the notes of all the birds.
To the predestinarian bird talk predestination,
To the bird with broken wings preach patience,
To the patient well-doer preach comfort and pardon,
To the spiritual 'Anka relate the glories of Mount Qaf,'
To the pigeon preach avoidance of the hawk,
To the lordly hawk mercy and self-control;
As for the bat, who lingers helpless in the dark,
Acquaint him with the society of the light;
To the fighting partridge teach peace,
To the cock the signs of dawning day.
In this way deal with all from the hoopoo to the eagle.

*Masnavi— Book 4: 2*

## Ready Cash

When a man acts basely towards Universal Reason,
Its form, the world, shows its teeth at him.
Be loyal to this father and renounce disobedience,
That this earthy house may furnish you golden carpets.
Then the judgment-day will be the "cash of your state,"
Earth and heavens will be transfigured before you.
I am ever in concord with this father of ours,
And earth ever appears to me as a Paradise.
Each moment a flesh form, a new beauty,
So that weariness vanishes at these ever-fresh sights.
I see the world filled with blessings,
Fresh waters ever welling up from new fountains.
The sound of those waters reaches my ears,
My brain and senses are intoxicated therewith.
Branches of trees dancing like fair damsels,
Leaves clapping hands like singers.
These glories are a mirror shining through a veil;
If the mirror were unveiled, how would it be?
I tell not one in a thousand of them,
Because every ear is stopped with doubt.
To men of illusions these tales are mere good tidings,
But men of knowledge deem them not tidings, but ready cash.

*Masnavi— Book 4: 8*

He is a letter to everyone.
You open it. It says, 'Live!'
— *Rumi*